THE ESSENTIAL BUYER'S GUIDE

FORD

MODEL A

All models 1927 to 1931

Your marque experts:
John Buckley & Mike Cobell

T0386533

VELOCE PUBLISHING
THE PUBLISHER OF FINE AUTOMOTIVE BOOKS

www.veloce.co.uk

First published in October 2018, reprinted December 2022 by Veloce Publishing Limited, Veloce House, Parkway Farm Business Park, Middle Farm Way, Poundbury, Dorchester, Dorset, DT1 3AR, England.
Telephone 01305 260068/Fax 01305 250479/email info@veloce.co.uk/web www.veloce.co.uk or www.velocebooks.com.
ISBN: 978-1-787112-70-4 UPC: 6-36847-01270-0

British Library Cataloguing in Publication Data – A catalogue record for this book is available from the British Library.
Typesetting, design and page make-up all by Veloce Publishing Ltd on Apple Mac.
Printed and bound by CPI Group (UK) Ltd, Croydon, CR0 4YY.

Front cover photograph courtesy John Barrett.

Introduction
– the purpose of this book

The Model A Ford was launched with much acclaim in late 1927, but volume production did not really get underway until 1928. It was somewhat old fashioned right from its inception, both stylistically and mechanically, but it sold well. However, 1930 saw sales begin to decline, and in late 1931 the car became obsolescent with the development of the Ford V8.

Despite the Model A's relatively short production period, over 5 million examples were produced. It was manufactured not only in the USA, but also at assembly factories in more than 20 other countries; it was the world's best-selling car, and the standard by which many others were judged.

The Model A was produced with an enormous range of different body styles. The basic mechanics, chassis, engine, gearbox, powertrain, front and rear axles, and brakes all remained pretty much the same. Ford's policy of continual development ensured that there were frequent minor changes as production continued but generally all the different mechanical parts of the Model A are interchangeable.

This book is not intended for those seeking the finer points of complete originality, nor for the exacting requirements of the concours d'elegance judge, but is here as an introduction to the pros and cons of ownership, the body styles likely to be encountered, what to anticipate when driving or maintaining it, and the mechanical points you should be aware of. It should also prove an essential pocket guide when inspecting a Model A prior to purchase, and thus help you decide whether to go-ahead and become the proud new owner, or simply walk away!

The Model A is an exceptionally strong, rugged vehicle. It has simple basic engineering throughout, and is reliable and affordable. With probably over 250,000 vehicles still in existence, the availability of both new and used spare parts is second to none. Parts availability alone has persuaded many enthusiasts to make it the old-timer car of their choice.

Against these good points, you need to consider that it is a cumbersome car. In its original form it is by no means an exhilarating drive, and though contemporary Ford advertisements claimed 65mph as the top speed, it is more likely that 40-50mph will be your comfortable maximum for cruising. However, with its antique braking, handling and steering, would you really want to travel much faster?

This was a car for the global market, and it is still found throughout the world. Reflecting that, in this book we have generally used the original US Ford terminology utilising British spelling. Where some of the words may be unfamiliar or ambiguous, we have initially put the alternative terms in brackets.

We would like to thank all the people involved in producing this book. The expertise, advice and friendship offered by members of the Model A Ford Club of Great Britain and other clubs throughout the world has been invaluable. We particularly wish to thank Jenny and Alf Anderson, Murray Ashby, Richard Forsyth, John and Gill Fishlock, Sammy Guthrie, and Nigel Stennet-Cox for reading through the drafts and providing many helpful suggestions.

John Buckley & Mike Cobell

Contents

THE ESSENTIAL BUYER'S GUIDE™ CURRENCY

At the time of publication a BG unit of currency "●" equals approximately US $1.00/GBP £0.83/Euro 0.96. Please adjust to suit current exchange rates using US dollar as the base currency. The cost of parts imported to Europe will often double due to shipping costs.

1 Is it the right car for you?
– marriage guidance

Although it is amongst the most practical of cars from its era, in the present day one cannot realistically consider the Model A Ford as a vehicle for everyday use.

Back in the 1920s and 1930s the roads were empty. Most local garages would be familiar with the A, and when things went wrong they could fix it for you there and then. Also, many roadside garages stocked a range of spare parts you might require. Nowadays, the roads are busy, out-of-town traffic speed is generally much greater, and other road users expect you to be able to stop on the proverbial dime.

Its size is a bonus for anyone looking to use it on a commercial basis for events such as weddings and school proms – in sedan (saloon) form, it can comfortably seat five people. One owner uses his as a profitable sideline taking picnic parties around scenic tourist areas.

The A is a wonderful car for touring and international classic car rallies. Its robustness has been proved in many adventures, and several have successfully completed the Peking-Paris and other challenging routes.

It is a popular car for vintage car competitions, such as navigation rallies or off-road trialling, and indeed it has almost become the car of choice for hill trials in the Vintage Sports Car Club in the UK.

The Model A lends itself to improved performance for speed events amongst the hotrod fraternity. Several specialist firms cater to this field.

Both the left-hand drive (LHD) and right-hand drive (RHD) versions exist.

1929 Model A Tudor fitted with sidelights.

The ideal car for tackling any sporting challenge. 1929 Roadster. (Courtesy Paul Sansom)

1928 Phaeton. Ready for hard work and adventures. (Courtesy Chris Batty)

However all the RHD versions had the accelerator pedal located centrally between the brake and the clutch pedals. Today this seems a most bizarre arrangement, but in its era this was fairly common, and the now conventional arrangement of clutch-

1930 Tudor. Polished for weddings.
(Courtesy Keith Evitts)

1930 Tudor at a rally checkpoint.
(Courtesy Paul Sansom)

Ample power: the Roadster with a rumble seat tows a caravan, whilst the Tudor follows with a trailer tent. The Model A Club of South Australia on tour. (Courtesy John Fishlock)

Recovery Truck, advertising and working. The car's commercial partner – the AA truck. (Courtesy John Cochran)

brake-accelerator did not become standard across all cars until towards the late 1930s. Many drivers of RHD Model As utilise the hand throttle in preference to the foot pedal, and if it gets all too worrying for you it is possible (at some expense) to reconfigure the central accelerator to normal layout.

The gearbox is a conventional 'crash' box with just three forward gears. It has no synchromesh, but is a relatively forgiving gearbox, and most people acquire the art of silent gear changing eventually.

The Model A is a straightforward car for the amateur mechanic, which is just as well, since most owners will need to be able to turn their hand at least to some routine maintenance. Not everyone has a sympathetic garage mechanic or knowledgeable friend close by.

Alternatives

Similar contemporary American cars such as Chrysler, Dodge and Chevrolet are more sophisticated mechanically, but are more expensive to buy, and parts availability is not as good as for the Model A. In the UK, some Morris and Austin cars of the Model A era are also worth considering, but compared with

Production of commercial variants of the Model A continued after 1931. This is a 1932 van. (Courtesy John Waterhouse)

the Ford they generally cost more, are heavier, have poorer performance and resourcing spare and replacement parts can be a problem.

All RHD models had a central accelerator. The brass pedal above the clutch is the starter button.

The Model A was produced for the world market. Many still earn their keep. (Courtesy Peter Cooper)

Extended wheelbase; Model A snack bar. (Courtesy Richard Forsyth)

1930 Coupé, International Maya Classic Rally in Panama. A car so simple to work on, the head gasket can be changed at the roadside, at night! (Courtesy Adrian Shooter)

1928 Phaeton. A profitable hobby – private hire with personal chauffeur. (Courtesy Steven White)

2 Cost considerations
– affordable, or a money pit?

Car purchase

The best guide to current prices for a Model A is to look in all the classic car magazines, club newsletters, and various websites. You will find some listed in chapter 17. The Model A has never commanded an astronomical price; it is one of the more affordable vintage cars. At the time of publishing, you can buy one that is useable but scruffy for about the price of a cheap modern saloon, yet for one in outstanding condition you need to budget no more than two or three times that. Over the years the value of the cars has steadily increased, but it would be imprudent to buy one solely as an investment. Nevertheless, the price for a Model A has generally kept up with inflation.

If you are intending to import a car, do not forget to add shipping costs, shipping insurance, dockside handling and storage, agency fees, as well as any import duties. It all adds up.

Parts availability is the best of any pre-1940 vehicle. Suppliers ship worldwide.

There is a plethora of handbooks and manuals available.

Tax & insurance

Most countries have a favourable road tax for collectors' cars; their annual mileage is usually substantially less than a modern vehicle.

Because it is relatively cheap to purchase and repair, insurance costs for the vehicle are low. Specialist insurers offer good deals, as do many clubs. It pays to ring round for insurance quotes. Expect to pay an annual premium of around 1-2% of the value of the car.

Fuel

Anticipate no more than 17-24mpg; less in hilly areas. There is no need to pay a premium for high octane fuel; the engine is basic and with its low revs and low compression ratio, it will run on ordinary standard octane fuel, with or without lead.

Home maintenance is straightforward – the only special tool needed for routine work is a hub puller, for access to the rear brake shoes.

Lubrication
This is not an expenditure worry unless you are unable to do it yourself and have to pay a professional.

Restoration and/or maintenance
Costs for labour will be the same as any other car.

Component price guide
These are the costs in US dollars (net of taxes and carriage), for components purchased in the USA. For other countries, anticipate paying approximately double to account for foreign shipping, import and local taxes. Prices are current at the time of going to press:

Cylinder head gasket ⬤x35
Engine gasket set ⬤x65
Pistons set ⬤x125
Timing gear ⬤x55
Valves (set of eight) ⬤x150
Radiator hose set ⬤x25
Front spring ⬤x150
Rear spring ⬤x400
High compression cylinder head ⬤x425
Points ⬤x20
Coil ⬤x20
New carburettor ⬤x510
Carburettor float ⬤x35
Generator (dynamo) exchange ⬤x220
Generator field coils ⬤x45
Clutch disc ⬤x40
Starter motor ⬤x220
Starter motor, modern pre-engaged ⬤x300
Exhaust manifold ⬤x100
Muffler (silencer) complete system ⬤x350
Front fender (wing) ⬤x450
Rear fender ⬤x360
Overdrive kit ⬤x3100
Front bumpers (chrome) ⬤x320
Wheel ⬤x460
Tyre (quality brand) ⬤x250
Tyre (budget range) ⬤x125
Inner tube ⬤x25
Professional full engine rebuild ⬤x5250

3 Living with a Model A
– will you get along together?

You're buying a slice of automotive history, so let's put that history in context.

Henry Ford introduced the Ford Model T in 1908, and it really did bring motoring to the millions. It was a breakthrough in design and construction when it first appeared and was the world's best-selling car, but by the mid 1920s other manufacturers had caught up. The Model T, with its familiar box shape styling, just two forward gears and primitive brakes, was now looking distinctly old-fashioned.

In 1926, plans were drawn up for a successor to the Model T, and during the following year the US factory was

The Model A's predecessor – the Ford Model T (1926 Coupé shown here). (Courtesy Michael Flather)

eventually shut down for six months to allow for complete retooling. Following a phenomenal promotional advertising campaign the New Ford – the Model A – was finally presented to the public in late 1927, though volume production did not really get under way until 1928.

The Model A was larger than its predecessor, its styling was more modern, though still the classic box-shape of the era. The engine produced 40bhp compared to the 20bhp of the Model T, even though it still had only four cylinders. It had a conventional gearbox, four wheel brakes, with a conventional distributor and coil ignition system.

The 1920s government of Great Britain (along with several other countries) was alarmed that sales of American cars were devastating its own automobile industries. It introduced swingeing road tax rates targeted at the large bore engines sent over from the USA. In 1910, the Royal Automobile Cub had devised a formula that had given an approximate horsepower of automobile engines of that time, without having to bench test them. By the 1920s engines had become much more efficient, but this RAC formula was still in use for annual road tax calculation:

$$hp = (D^2 \times n)/2.5$$

(Where D=the diameter of the cylinder in inches, and n=the number of cylinders.)

In 1927, the small-bore Austin 7

The only external way of telling if it's a small bore or large bore engine. Large bore (shown here) does not have a 'land' between cylinders 1-2 and 3-4 ...

... while the small bore engine has a space that almost accomodates a UK penny (2cm diameter).

was charged only £8 per annum, whereas the Ford Model T was being taxed at £23pa. The bigger-bore engine of the new Model A would have been taxed even more. To ameliorate this potentially disastrous situation, a smaller bore version of the Model A engine (2043cc) rated at RAC 14.9hp was initially used for the British Model A. Other countries with a similar taxation regime also used the small bore engine. In Great Britain at that time, commercial vehicles were taxed on a different basis, so they normally used the 200.5cu in (3285cc) engine (RAC rated at 24hp). From 1930 onward, the larger engine was available as an alternative for British Model A cars, but Ford's sales of the Model A in Britain were by now not far short of calamitous. The company's problems were compounded by the £5m capital cost of the new Dagenham factory, and the Ford Motor Company Ltd, which was the British arm of the Ford empire, was at this stage close to bankruptcy. Sensibly, it was decided to concentrate Dagenham's output on the new Model Y and commercial vehicles only. This policy turned around the fortunes of Ford in Britain; the commercials sold well, and became common on all the roads, whilst the Model Y went on to become Britain's best-selling car.

At the end of 1931 the Model A was discontinued in the USA. However, some foreign plants continued Model A production in car, van and truck guises even as late as the 1950s.

The Model A was superseded by the V8 and the Model B. The V8 attracted a high level of road tax in many countries, and was thirsty on fuel, so for many people the Model B was the preferred choice. The Model B had a more modern body than the Model A, but it lost its distinguishing feature of the exposed radiator. The engine of the Model B was still a 4-cylinder, side valve, 3285cc unit, very much based on the Model A with many engine components interchangeable. It had better valve timing, the oil system

The Ford Model B.
(Courtesy D Wilson-Green)

The Ford V8. The great leap forward, rendering the A, the B, and many other cars obsolete (picture shows 1935 model). (Courtesy Adrian Shooter)

pressure-fed the main bearings, and it produced 50bhp compared to the Model A's 40bhp. A small bore version of the Model B engine was available in countries where road tax was an issue. Many Model As have been retrospectively fitted with the superior Model B engine.

The truck and van business
Ford produced millions of Model A cars, but it also realised that the business sector was a market that it could successfully exploit. Commercial variants, vans, and trucks came in an enormous variety of body styles, wheelbase length, and single or twin axle configurations. They had the same 3285cc engine as the car but the suspension was much stronger and the rear axle ratio was lower. Trucks came with the nomenclature AA or BB. Restoration of these commercial vehicles today attracts a strong following.

The chrome lever on the left of the steering column is for ignition advance/retard. Push up to retard; down to advance. The lever on the right is the hand throttle. Centre steering wheel is horn button and lighting switch. 1928 model shown here.

In line with Ford's policy of continual development during the Model As production run there were many minor changes to various components but the only major alteration was in 1930 when the car had a make-over, the radiator became taller, wheels became 19 inch instead of 21 inch, an improved steering box fitted and the body had a re-style to make it look marginally more modern. Thus there is a noticeable change in style, if not mechanics, between the 1927-1929 models and the 1930-1931 versions.

The bodies for cars were made by Ford in-house, and also by Murray, Briggs, and local coachbuilding firms.

All Model A Ford cars were based on the same frame/chassis, engine and power train.

In, out and under the car
Many of the cars had non-adjustable seats, but nowadays seat-adjusting kits can be bought. Some cars are particularly awkward as the front bench seat cannot be moved at all, kit or no kit! The seats in all the Model As are comfortable and generous, but some find the driving position rather cramped.

The dash panel has just an ignition switch, ammeter, dash light, fuel gauge and speedo.

On the steering column are two levers. The left controls the advance/

A restyled dash panel with a round speedo was introduced in late 1930. (Courtesy Alan Crossland)

retard of the ignition, and must be adjusted to suit the revs and the engine load; this is no hardship, and is part of the fun of driving an A. The right hand lever is a hand throttle. Centre of the steering wheel has the horn and light switch.

The body of the open cars in particular are liable to flex, and extra safety catches on the doors are sensible.

The Model A has a gravity scuttle-mounted fuel tank, and this is a structural component of the body. The Model B has a conventional rear-mounted tank with mechanical pump.

The windshields (windscreen) of all As were made of safety glass, even in 1927, but not all cars had safety glass in the side and rear windows. Most, but not all cars by now have been rebuilt with safety glass in place. Every pane of glass is flat, so replacement is relatively straightforward.

No seatbelts originally, of course, but it is feasible to fit simple lap belts, and with ingenuity lap and diagonal belts can be installed.

The brakes are rod operated on all 4 wheels and adequate when well set up. A firm pressure is needed to operate them.

Many modifications are available for the Model A such as overdrive, high compression head, hydraulic brakes, modern starter motors, alternators and telescopic shock absorbers to replace the rather ineffective standard lever arm ones. Turn-signal kits are a useful addition. The electrics were originally 6V and if kept in good order perform well, nevertheless many As are converted to 12V. Not all modifications improve the vehicle.

Starting
An A starts easily; fuel tap on, ignition on, enrich the Gas Adjusting Valve (mixture control) using one full turn if a cold start, hand throttle set to fast idle, ignition lever set to retard, choke knob also pulled upwards if a cold start, and then press the floor-mounted starter switch. Once it fires, immediately release the choke.

On the road
Select first, ease out the clutch pedal whilst increasing the revs, and away we go. Gently change into second gear and subsequently into third (top gear) at about 18mph. Adjust the ignition timing lever as needed.

Handling is adequate for a car of its size, but it is certainly not 'sporty.'

Maintenance
Oil changes are needed every 1200 miles. Opinions vary on the best oil to use, but most owners are happy with 20/50 multigrade or straight 30 mineral. Also, several places need greasing every few hundred miles. The contact points may need occasional cleaning and resetting.

The gear box and back axle are fairly strong, but checking their oil levels should be routine.

Tools
The threads are mostly UNC or UNF; a set of AF spanners is needed in the workshop. Special tools generally aren't essential, though a hub-puller may be needed to access the rear brake shoes.

Over 50 different varieties of body were available. The commonest ones (available in both the 1927-1929 and 1930-1931 versions) are:

Tudor Two–door sedan (saloon) that can accommodate five adults. It is probably the strongest of all the body styles, being an all-steel structure except for the roof. The roof on Model A Tudors, Fordors and Coupés was artificial leather fabric, which was padded underneath with wadding, in turn supported by a wire mesh and wood ribs running transversely.

'Artificial leather' roof of the Tudor.

Fordor Four-door sedan which, though similar in style to the Tudor, had a body built as a wooden framework to which panels were affixed.

Phaeton Four-door five-seater open tourer, with a fabric top that could be lowered and clip-on sidescreens that could be removed completely.

Coupé Two-seater with a trunk (boot), which had the option of a rumble seat for the hardy (or the mother in law).

Sports Coupé Similar to a closed Coupé; a two-seater, two-door closed car, but with a fabric roof that resembles a convertible. However, the roof doesn't fold down – it just looks sporty!

Roadster Similar to the Coupé, but a convertible in which the fabric roof could be lowered and side screens completely removed, if weather permitted.

1929 Fordor. The radiator stone guard is an extra. (Courtesy Jon Davidson)

Cabriolet Similar to the Roadster but a little more refined as the windows were glass that could be rolled (wound) down into the door panel.

1930-31 green Coupé. Rear compartment for luggage or the mother-in-law. (Courtesy Richard Forsyth)

Show standard 1929 Phaeton. Stone guard and side mount spare wheel were extras. (Courtesy Richard Forsyth)

1928/29 Sport Coupé. The Sports Coupé had a rumble seat and pram irons. The hood is fixed, and cannot be lowered. (Courtesy George Langton)

Deluxe versions were available. These generally had minor luxury touches added to enhance their desirability and increase their price. One noticeable exception to the minor detailing normally associated with the deluxe range was the Phaeton. The body of the Deluxe Phaeton was structurally different, as it was a two-door with a lowered windshield height, and tilting front seat to allow rear passenger access.

Pick-up As it is based on the car chassis, this is a very popular collectors' vehicle today. Some Pick-ups had an open cab with a fabric top, and from late 1928 a fully closed steel cab was added to the range. The radiator surround and headlights shells were painted black.

Station Wagon (Woodie) Originally made only by third party builders, these were available from the factory from 1929.

Speedsters were never an official factory offering, but specialist builders could purchase the running chassis (which included the hood (bonnet) and cowl sections) from Ford, and then add whatever the customer required. Turning a car into a Speedster, by ridding it of its dishevelled bodywork and fitting one of the proprietary Speedster kits, was (and still is) a relatively cheap and quick way to get back on the road.

1930-31 Roadster. The rear compartment /trunk can carry luggage or be fitted with a 2 person rumble seat. This is a Deluxe version which came with luggage rack, side-mount spare wheel and rumble seat already fitted. (Courtesy George Langton)

1929 Pick-up. These were a cheap vehicle originally. (Courtesy Mark Perkins)

1928-29 Station Wagon. Familiarly known as the 'Woodie.' (Courtesy Richard Bell)

Speedster – exciting, unprotected motoring, and a quick way of getting a rolling chassis back on the road. (Courtesy Stephen Longden)

1930 AA flat bed truck. (Courtesy Bonhams)

Much of the Model A's value depends on condition. A car that is immediately usable on the road will command a higher price than one that needs work on it even if the seller says it only needs a 'light re-commissioning.' One that is obviously cared for and in sound condition will be pricier than one that has severe rust issues or a mechanical problem.

Left is a late 1931 slant window Fordor; right a 1930 Fordor. (Courtesy Richard Smoothy)

The biggest change during the Model A's production was the alteration of the body style in 1930 to make it a slightly smoother looking car. At the same time, an improved steering box was introduced. Nevertheless, side by side, the early cars and later cars still look remarkably similar, and both remain unmistakable Model As.

The various models had each a strong following: Tudors for their indestructibility, Phaetons and Roadsters for fresh air excitement. Cabriolets are probably the most expensive.

Originality is often sought. However, it is rare to come across a Model A that has not been rebuilt at some time in its life. Beware of cars that are advertised as 'completely original barn-find,' as these are rarely completely original. Many of these were used and fettled in a good, bad or indifferent manner during their working life, after which they may have been put into storage because of a major mechanical problem. Of course, there are some true 'sleeping beauties' waiting to be brought back to life.

Taking as datum a Model A with excellent mechanicals, body and interior which has won a major national concours competition, the following are approximate value guides

Very good with no faults **75%**
Tidy usable with nothing fundamentally wrong **50%**
A tatty but usable example **40%**
A non-runner, all pieces present **25%**

5 Before you view
– be well informed

To avoid a wasted journey, and the disappointment of finding that the car does not match your expectations, it will help if you're very clear about what questions you want to ask before you pick up the telephone. Some of these points might appear basic, but when you're excited about the prospect of buying your dream classic, it's amazing how some of the most obvious things slip the mind – make a list, and join an owners club in advance!

Where is the car?
Is it going to be worth travelling a long distance, or even across a border? A locally advertised car, although it may not sound very interesting, can add to your knowledge for very little effort, so make a visit.

Dealer or private sale
Establish if the car is being sold by its owner or by a trader. A private owner should have all the history, so don't be afraid to ask detailed questions. A dealer may have more limited knowledge of a car's history, but should at least have some information. Cars of this age do not normally carry any warranty, but ask anyway and get a printed copy. A dealer may also offer finance.

Cost of collection and delivery
Unless you buy the car very close to home, it's likely you'll want it transported to you. The seller may be able to arrange or quote for delivery by car transporter, or even drive it home for you. Several specialist classic car transport firms advertise on the web and in magazines.

View – when and where
It is always preferable to view at the vendor's home or business premises. In the case of a private sale, the car's documentation should tally with the vendor's name and address. If buying from a dealer the documents may show the owner's, not the dealer's details, if the seller's name and address does not match owner's details ask about this and assure yourself that everything is legitimate. Arrange to view only in daylight and avoid a wet day. Most cars look better in poor light or when wet.

Reason for sale
Ask why is the car being sold and how long has it been with the current owner? Details like how many previous owners, mileage, service history etc are not so relevant on a car of this age.

Left-hand drive or right-hand drive?
The choice is yours since the Ford factories built thousands of each. With so many factory built ones available there is normally no need to contemplate conversion.

Modifications
Is the car absolutely standard? Are there any modifications that add or detract to its value for you?

Condition (body/frame/interior/mechanicals)

Ask for an honest appraisal of the car's condition. Ask specifically about some of the check items described in chapter 7.

Matching data/legal ownership

One idiosyncrasy of the Model A is that the original frame (chassis) number is not visible unless you strip the body completely off the frame, and with the age of the vehicle the number may no longer be legible. Some of the assembly

The engine number is located on the left-hand side, above the block water inlet.

plants did not stamp the frame at all! Initially this caused no problem, as the engine number was used as the ID of the vehicle. But of course changing an engine would produce a new engine number, but not a new frame number. To overcome this hiccup many countries and states introduced their own VIN numbering of the A and issued an official authority-recognized vehicle identification number. You may (or may

The letters 'CA' indicates this engine was made in Canada.

not) find a plate with this on the firewall (bulkhead).

Sometimes on rebuilding an engine the engine number was ground off! Your car may not have its original engine anyway. The outcome of all this is that you cannot judge the year of a Model A by the engine number nor by the VIN number as shown in the registration document. Check the car against the photos in this book to gauge the year of it. Be happy that the vehicle and documents tally as far as possible, if in doubt walk away or contact one of the owners' clubs for advice.

Even if the car does not legally need roadworthiness certification, a document showing roadworthiness by an independent professional is reassuring.

Does the car have current road licence/tax?

Does the vendor own the car outright? Money might be owed to a finance company or bank: the car could even be stolen. Several organizations will supply the data on ownership, based on the car's licence plate number, for a fee. Such companies can also tell you whether the car has been written off by an insurance company. In the UK, for example, HPI, AA and RAC can supply vehicle data. Most other countries will have similar organisations.

How you can pay

A cheque will take several days to clear and until cleared the seller is unlikely to relinquish the car. Cash gives an immediate transaction as does a banker's draft (a cheque issued by a bank) which is as good as cash, but safer. Online bank transfers are acceptable to all parties.

Professional vehicle check

It is unlikely any professional will have sufficient knowledge to check the car unless he is a specialist for this particular marque. A call to one of the Model A clubs may put you in touch with a knowledgeable enthusiast who could help you.

6 Inspection equipment
– these items will really help

Before you rush out of the door, gather together a few items that will help as you work your way around the car. This book is designed to be your guide at every step, so take it along and use the check boxes to help assess each area of the car you're interested in. Don't be afraid to let the seller see you using it.

This book
Reading glasses (if you need them for close work)
Magnet (not powerful, a fridge magnet is ideal)
Flashlight
Probe (a small screwdriver works very well)
Overalls
Mirror on a stick
Camera and selfie stick to photograph underside of vehicle
A friend, preferably with good Model A Ford knowledge.
Jack
Axle stands
Disposable gloves

Inspection kit. Take a friend also.

The A weighs around 1000kg (approximately 1 ton), and requires a strong trailer and tow car. (Courtesy Trevor Bainbridge)

Take your glasses if you need them to read the documents and close up inspections.

A magnet will help you check if the car is full of filler, or has fibreglass fenders which are a cheaper option than metal ones for rebuilds. If you think other areas may have filler use the magnet to check but take care not to scratch the paint. Expect to find a little filler here and there on some cars.

A flashlight with fresh batteries will be useful for peering into the wheelarches and under the car.

A small screwdriver can be used – with care – as a probe. With this you should be able to check an area of severe corrosion, but be careful: if it's really bad the screwdriver might go right through the metal!

Be prepared to get dirty. Take along a pair of overalls, if you have them. Fixing a mirror at an angle on the end of a stick may seem odd, but you'll want to check the underside of the vehicle and it will also help you to peer into some of the important crevices. It is possible to crawl under a Model A without jacking it up but if you want to raise it off the ground to make things easier use axle stands and make sure it is absolutely safe before going under.

Take lots of photos, you can study the photos at leisure later and if any part of the car causes you concern, seek a friend's view. A second opinion is invaluable.

7 Fifteen minute evaluation

– walk away or stay?

The priority is to check that the car is what it claims to be. Indeed, a lot of this chapter can be covered by a detailed conversation over the phone, and by studying quality photos from the vendor. First, you need to check that it is indeed a legitimate Model A Ford. Look at the body; then the engine bay. Have a quick look under the car at the rear axle, suspension and steering. Are all these major components correct, and do they correspond with what the car claims to be?

Look at the body again. Check that it is as described – a genuine Tudor, or a genuine Cabriolet etc. It is not unknown for some saloon cars to have had their roof cut off in order to masquerade as a factory produced convertible tourer.

Use the photos in this book to check the approximate year of manufacture: is it the 1928-1929 version of the Model A or the 1930-1931 version with the larger radiator? The wheels of the 1928-1929 models were 21in with a small hub cap. The later 1930-1931 versions had 19in wheels and larger hub caps. Any wheels other than these are non-originals, and, though later wheels and tyres may improve the handling, they also devalue the vehicle.

Check the tyres for consistency of make and how much tread is left on them. Ask the vendor if he knows how old the tyres are.

Briefly walk around the car and view it looking along the length. Do the panels appear straight without any dents? Have the doors sagged? Unless fully rebuilt, some sag is inevitable on cars this old.

Stand back and view the car from the front. Are the headlights the correct style, in the correct place and with the

1927-1929 cars had 21in wheels with small hub caps. (Courtesy Caroline Gilchrist)

1930-31 cars had 19in wheels with larger hub caps. (Courtesy John Richardson)

1927-29 radiator and surround.

1930 and later models had the taller radiator. (Courtesy Richard Bell)

correct light bar? Does the radiator appear correct? Is the radiator surround in acceptable condition? 1928-1929 cars had nickel plated radiators; the later models stainless steel.

View the car from the back. Is the rear axle the correct type? Does the car lean to one side? Many do, as over the decades the mainspring weakens.

Check each front fender to ensure it is metal, and feel or magnet-test for filler at the front peak and outer edge where they are prone to rust. Some filler is acceptable – in any case it is unlikely that any original wings have survived intact for more than 80 years. Look carefully for cracks where the headlight bar enters the front fender. Cracks are also common on the edge of the fender where it flexes. Sometimes these have been reinforced with a metal plate secured by two large bolts.

Similarly, check the same places on the rear fenders. The rear ones are renowned for stress cracking at the edge after decades of use. Check the running boards, especially where they join the rear fender: this is a well known rust trap.

Look at the right-hand side of the engine. Has it got the original style of cylinder head or does it have an aftermarket one? Is the carburettor the correct cast iron Zenith type? Many cars now have an alloy Tillotson carb.

Are the distributor and plug leads the correct style?

Late 1931 Fordor. In 1931, the style of the A changed, acquiring a slanted windshield and losing the visor above it. (Courtesy Richard Smoothy)

The circular fitting in the firewall near the sediment bowl was for a cabin heater from the manifold.

Look at the left side of the engine. Does it have the correct generator (dynamo) and cutout or has it been replaced with a modern alternator?

Is the starter the original type? Does the wiring in the engine bay look in good condition? Pull the dip stick. Is the oil fresh or is it black, indicating maybe a worn engine or just in need of TLC and an oil change. Any sign of water in the oil could indicate a leaking head gasket.

A later post-production distributor with HT leads, rather than the original simple metal strips. (Courtesy Mark Perkins)

Also check for evidence of severe oil leaks (though all Model As leak to some extent) and check for coolant leaks, from the head gasket, water pump, hoses and radiator.

If there is a chance that this could be one of the small bore engines check that the engine is the size it claims to be.

Open and close all the doors to check that they fit neatly and firmly.

Are the seats the correct ones for the car, or have some others been fitted at some stage? What condition is the upholstery and the door panels? If it's a closed car what condition is the headlining? Staining may indicate a leaking roof. If there are glass windows can they all be opened as they should be?

What condition is the paint finish of the interior – the dash rail, the fuel tank and the interior garnish rails along the bottom edge of the windows? Have any extra switches or gauges been added to the car. Many have an oil pressure gauge and temperature gauge attached to the steering column.

Cracks on the rear fender.

Not all cracks are this obvious.

Does the horn button work the horn? And is it the proper horn?

Check the steering column light switch works correctly, and check all the exterior lights work.

Get the vendor to start the engine. Ford As start easily, though the starter on the original 6V system turns it over very slowly.

Look at the engine bay again – does it look as you'd expect it to?

Stand back and take a long hard

The horn push associated with the improved two-tooth steering box of later models.

Quail mascot. Early radiator surrounds were nickel plated and liable to pitting, and rust with age. 1930-31 cars had stainless steel surrounds.

Cowl lights are common – often used as turn signals or parking lights.

look at the car. Is this a car you'd like to own, or is it time to say 'Thank you' and walk away?

Unless you've already rejected it, now is the time to check paperwork. Look at the registration documents and make sure these tally with the car, are the engine and identification numbers correctly recorded? If the car has been recently imported does it have the correct export and import documents? If it is not registered for use on the road – either because it is registered with the licensing authority as statutory off-road notification, or perhaps because it's

Look along the waistline to check the doors for fit and droop.

spent many years as a museum exhibit you need to find out if getting it street legal will be straightforward. An owners' club may be able to help you with this.

Does it have a roadworthiness certificate, and when and where was this granted? Does it have any authentication/heritage certificate from a recognised owners' club or other authority? What's the history of the car? Can the verbal history be supported with written evidence? If the vendor states that he rebuilt it, ask to have a look at the photographic record.

Check exactly what the car is. Are the key components consistent with the claimed model and date of manufacture?

Does the official paperwork match the vehicle, and is this adequate to allow usage in your country/state?

Has it got the correct body, or has it been altered in some way? If you are looking for a hot rod, this is not the book for you.

What non-standard components and features does the car have? For example, high compression head, hydraulic brakes, alternator, automatic advance distributor, electronic ignition, overdrive, Do these make it more usable? Do these detract from its appeal for you? Do they impinge on the value? Would it be difficult or expensive to return the car to original spec?

Is the body sound? Do the mechanicals appear in good condition?

Are there any areas of severe rust? Look particularly at the fenders, under the car at the rear floor area, base of doors and side panels where they join the splash shields above the running board.

Does your local or national Model A Owners' club know this car or owner?

For you, is it a feasible and financially viable proposition?

Is it really what you're looking for? How about walking away, as plenty of others will come on the market?

The left side of the engine in a RHD car. A tidy, not concours, engine bay, with some modern wiring showing at the cutout sitting on the generator, and a black safety fuse visible above the starter motor.

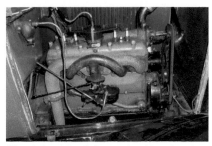

The right side of the engine bay showing the correct Zenith carb. The fuel pipe should not dip below the carb. The distributor has a brown bakelite body (they are normally black). The spark plugs have the correct clips, though the HT lead should be black.

Looking at the rear seats of a LHD Tudor. The passenger seat folds forward for easy access, and there is more space in the back than many modern cars. Basic re-upholstery of the seats and side panels is fairly straightforward, but new headlinings require much time and effort.

Score each section using the boxes as follows: 4 = excellent; 3 = good; 2 = average; 1 = poor. The totting up procedure is detailed at the end of the chapter. Be realistic in your marking!

You are buying a Model A because you want a historic car, not because you need one. The market for Model As is active – they are not rare, and if the one you're looking at doesn't fit most of the criteria you've drawn up, then it is easy to walk away and start investigating others that might be more to your liking.

Don't take any risks if you jack up the car. Always make sure it is safely and securely supported on axle stands, with the wheels chocked to prevent the car moving.

Before the test drive
General appearance and fit of panels

4 ☐ 3 ☐ 2 ☐ 1 ☐

Look along each side for any dings or dents. Look at the fit of the hood against the scuttle petrol tank and the radiator surround. Recheck each door for opening/closing, and view the waistline to check for any sagging of the doors.

The fenders and splash shields of all the Model A cars were black. The body was available in a variety of colours, which changed from year to year as well as from country to country. Colour matching for any respray of individual panels can be tricky, as colours will have faded over time. Fortunately, the Model A has several 'shut' lines making the job a little less tiresome. The waistline of the sedans is often highlighted with coach lining. Over the decades, deviation from the original colour scheme has become inevitable.

Suspicious filler on the outside bottom edge of the door.

Rust visible underneath the door.

Brake and tail light. Repro parts are not always of the highest quality.

Brightwork-nickel/chrome/stainless steel

4 ☐ 3 ☐ 2 ☐ 1 ☐

Early cars mostly use nickel plating for the brightwork, but from 1929 onwards more use was made of chrome. Chrome plating was more durable and shinier than nickel.

Inspect all the chrome and nickel work for peeling. 1927-29 cars generally had nickel plated radiator surrounds (though those of very late 1929 may be chrome

Small tears can be repaired.

plated). For the revised larger radiator 1930-1931 model, the radiator surround was stainless steel. Bumper bars can pit with rust or peel unless they are later stainless steel ones. New bumpers are available, and it can be cheaper to buy new ones rather than have existing ones replated, but obviously at some loss of originality. The headlamp bowls of the early Model As were nickel plated and can pit; later ones were stainless steel. The reflectors of the lamps can suffer from rust pitting.

Rust on the 1928-1929 hub caps. 1930-1931 hub caps were stainless.

Chrome pitting and peeling at back of bumpers. Stainless steel ones can be purchased.

Lens patterns vary – check they match.

Roof

For sedans, check there are no cuts to the fabric of the roof, and that it has a reasonable seal against the metal sections. In addition, inspect the firmness of the gutters along the sides, and make sure these are securely affixed. On soft tops, erect and lower the top, checking everything links together properly. Also fit all the sidescreens and check their attachment to the body. Inspect the outside of the tops and sidescreens for staining or rot. New frames and new soft tops are available.

Windshield (windscreen)

The windshield was originally safety glass. Do check that all the glass in the car is either laminated or tempered safety glass. A glass manufacturer's logo etched in somewhere may indicate it's safety glass of one type or the other. In the absence of any marking, look at the edge of the glass to check. Laminated glass will be obvious by the two sheets sandwiching a thin plastic film. Also, laminated glass often shows extra reflections; try placing a coin on the glass or holding a cigarette lighter flame near it and studying the resulting images. Tempered glass is harder to verify – viewing tempered glass through Polaroid spectacles will often show it having alternating light and dark areas.

Laminated glass is obvious if you can see the edge.

Laminated glass can also be detected by multiple reflections close up.

The wiper is usually just a single one in front of the driver, and either hand operated, electric operated or vacuum operated depending on the year, model and international variations. Many people have fitted twin wipers for their passenger's benefit.

Engine bay inspection

Check the engine is correct, and if there's a chance that it might be the small bore (2043cc) version check by looking at the left side of the block. The 'land' between cylinders 1 and 2, and cylinders 3 and 4 (see Chapter 3) is non-existent on the large bore version; the small bore version has a flat area between the curvature of these cylinders.

Look at the cylinder head and head gasket joint; minor coolant seepage often occurs here, but so long as the car performs well this is of no significance. Does it look as though the previous owner took pride in what goes on under the hood, or is there evidence of neglect? Is the oil clean and at the correct level? Is the sediment bowl at the top of the fuel pipe clear? Is the wiring tidy? Is there any sign of serious oil or coolant leak? Does the exhaust system look in good condition? Are the generator, the distributor and the carburettor the correct types?

Radiator

Check the radiator for any obvious signs of damage. Sometimes a few fins are slightly out of true, and the inside fins just in front of the fan have minor bending where people have been tightening or refitting waterpumps and fans.

The fan on a Model A should have two blades. It is prone to rusting, weakening and fracturing, with catastrophic results. Unless the fan is new, budget for its replacement as one of the first jobs to undertake if you buy the car. Some Model As are fitted with radiator shrouds (cowls) which improve the efficiency of the fan.

Fender cracks

Look again at each fender for cracks at the edge and where the light bar is attached. A simple remedy can be the addition of patch brackets and bolts.

Rust

Generally the Model A isn't a rot box – the frame rarely suffers from rust – but check the lower edge of each door, and the lower edge of the scuttle side panel. The fenders are prone to rust at the forward peak, along the edges of the wheelarches where the metal is folded over and also where it is attached to the running board.

Look for corrosion on the windshield surround.

With a light, crawl under the car to check the rear crossmember at the bottom of the outer body panel, and also the rear floor panel just in front of it. If too far gone for repair, replacement crossmembers can be bought as a complete unit ready to fit.

The rear fender/running board joint is another potential rust area.

A vulnerable rust area – the rear floor viewed from the underside.

Rusting of the rear floor area can look worrying, but it is not structural, and repairs are within the remit of a good home mechanic. Check the running board for rigidity.

Wheels

Check they are the correct wheels for the year. Be aware that the very early Model As had particular wheels and hubs, retrospectively known as AR wheels. Unlike all the other wheels and hubs, which are completely interchangeable throughout the years, the AR wheels are absolutely specific. They are NOT interchangeable with any of the later hubs and wheels; you cannot mix a later wheel with an AR hub, nor vice-versa. Check the spokes of each wheel by visual inspection and by tapping them – if faulty, they emit

Checking wheel run-out. No high-tech needed.

a different sound to the rest.

Look for welds on wheel. (21-inch wheels are more vulnerable.)

Inside the wheel, welds are obvious.

The spokes are not threaded with a nipple at the end; each spoke on the Model A wheel is welded to both rim and center hub. If you wish to check the lateral run-out for trueness of each wheel, jack the wheel and spin it. Being ⅛-inch out of true is well within acceptable limits. Whilst spinning the wheel, listen for any rust particles that may be in the hollow rim. Also listen for any rumble from wheel bearings.

Tyres

Whatever the brand of tyre, they must not only have legal tread depth, but also be free of serious sidewall cracks. Remember to check the inside sidewall, too! All Model As originally had blackwall tires, though whitewalls are a popular aftermarket styling enhancement. Tyres do have an age limit, but laws differ in various countries. So if in any doubt, budget for a new set.

Steering and front axle

With the car resting on the ground, check for rotational play of the steering wheel – having such a large steering wheel exaggerates things, and most Model As have no less than 2 inches of slack. This slackness can be anywhere in the system from the steering box to the wheels. Try and establish where the play is – steering box, pitman arm (drop arm), drag link, trackrods etc, by firmly grasping each in turn, pushing and pulling it whilst looking for any play.

The trackrod ends and drag link ends are spring loaded and adjustable. Steering boxes can be rebuilt, as all the parts are available. Check the steering for axial play (up and down) – there should be none. Try to 'rock' the steering wheel to check for shaft bearing wear.

Grease is preferable to rust. Regular greasing is essential for longevity.

Jack up the front axle, secure it with axle stands, and check the spindle bolts (king pins) for wear by trying to rock the top of the wheel in and out. Replacement spindle bolt kits are available. The front wheel bearings are easily adjusted or replaced, if necessary.

Braking system

Ideally there should be approx 1in of travel on the foot brake pedal before resistance is felt. The pedal shouldn't go all the way to the floor! Ensure that it returns to its correct position after being depressed.

Check both the brake and clutch pedals for excessive lateral wobble, in which case re-bushing on the shaft is required. Apply the emergency/parking handbrake lever to ensure the pawl and ratchet engage well. Go under the car and look at the brake rods. Ideally there should be no play at any of the clevis pins. Over many decades the holes

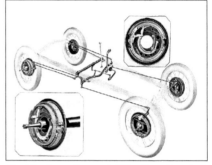

Rod brakes all round. Effective stopping for the era. This diagram shows the later brake system.

for the clevis pins enlarge and become oval. There should be an anti-rattler pull-off spring attached to the frame for each rod. New brake rods, clevis pins and anti-rattler pull-off springs are easily installed.

The peculiarity of the very early cars with the AR wheels was that the emergency brake used the same rods as the service brake (foot brake); it was not a completely independent system. Thus for this early brake system efficiency is absolutely essential. Ensure it is working correctly, as there is really no second system in reserve unlike the Model T.

Check for any significant oil leaking from the brake drums.

Hydraulic brakes, though non-original, can improve braking performance. Various kits have been around for many years, and be aware that new seals/hoses or other replacement parts will be required at some time. Make sure you know what brand of hydraulic system it is, and ideally the part numbers and where replacement parts are available.

Once wiped of mud, any patches and repairs to the wheelarch can be seen.

Restored wheelarch. Note the aftermarket 'dog bone' shock absorber link. (Courtesy Fred Vaccaro Jr)

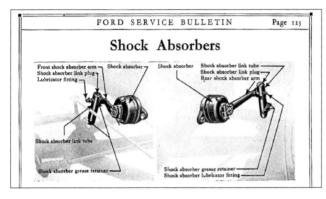

Original shock absorber links require greasing.

Suspension and shock absorbers

Check the car sits well and the springs appear in good condition. The shock absorbers are lever arm, and are expensive. Some Model As have been retrospectively fitted with modern shock absorbers. A few cars – particularly those from South America – have had all four removed entirely and no replacement fitted at all. Some people find that they have no effect, others swear they are essential!

Check the front and rear springs. The shackles at each end should appear well greased. The top of each spring is hidden in the channel of the crossmember, but check the springs as far as possible for any broken leaves. Replacement springs are available. Different vehicles had different numbers of leaves depending on the overall weight, or expected load.

Starting the car and the test drive

Ask the vendor to start the car. The road test is best carried out by someone with experience of driving a Model A Ford.

Starting the engine and idling

The Model A should always start easily. There is a good solid 'clunk' as the bendix of the starter motor engages with the starter ring of the flywheel. Even when very cold, the engine should generally start within five revolutions. Once started adjust the hand throttle and turn the mixture control clockwise to settle the idle, which should become steady after about 30 seconds. If starting from warm, usually no choke or enrichment is needed. A warm engine should tick over at about 360-500rpm.

Electrics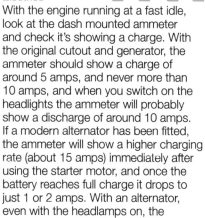

With the engine running at a fast idle, look at the dash mounted ammeter and check it's showing a charge. With the original cutout and generator, the ammeter should show a charge of around 5 amps, and never more than 10 amps, and when you switch on the headlights the ammeter will probably show a discharge of around 10 amps. If a modern alternator has been fitted, the ammeter will show a higher charging rate (about 15 amps) immediately after using the starter motor, and once the battery reaches full charge it drops to just 1 or 2 amps. With an alternator, even with the headlamps on, the ammeter should not show a discharge.

The 'Powerhouse Generator' was fitted on early models. (Courtesy John Richardson)

If the original generator has been fitted with a regulator instead of a cutout, the charging rate will be about 5-10 amps until fully charged, when it should drop to about 1-2 amps. The simplest way of checking that the generator or alternator is working is to simply rev up the engine speed from idle – if the headlights go brighter, the generator's working! Whatever system the car is fitted with, the main priority is that the battery gets charged, and the battery and electric system hold their charge when switched off!

Properly maintained, the original 6V system is adequate, but many owners convert to 12V. The batteries for 12V are cheaper, and it offers a greater potential range of additional accessories such as

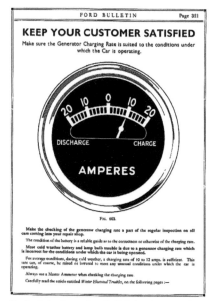

Period dealer advert. Original generators with cut outs are reliable, but batteries last longer if the charging rate is normally kept below 5 amps.

turn signals or more powerful lights. New and rebuilt generators and alternators are available for both 6 and 12V. If the car has been converted to 12V, the starter will usually turn the engine noticeably faster. Originally the A had only one rear tail light, but most now have two to meet modern legislation. Originally, the Model A had no fuses whatsoever. As a sensible safety measure, many have retrospectively been fitted with a fuse (normally 35 amps). Often you will find this is attached to the top of the starter motor. A battery master cut-off switch is a good idea.

On the move
Clutch   ④ ③ ② ①
Cars before late 1928 usually had a multi-plate clutch; later cars a singleplate. It is difficult to identify which a car has without lifting the carpet and floor board or plate to access the inspection cover in the flywheel housing (bell housing). The inspection covers for multi-plate clutches are wider than they are tall, for single-plate ones they are taller than they are wide! If all that is too confusing and you've got as far as looking at the inspection cover, you may want to undo the bolts holding it and take a peek to confirm. Also, usually with the single-plate clutch, the rear underside of the flywheel housing has two ribs, whereas the multi-plate has none. Multi-plate

clutches can suffer from some clutch judder, but so can single-plate clutches if they are not true. Complete single-plate clutches with clutch housing and disc can be purchased new, but only used parts are available for multi-plate clutches. The flywheel housing is different for the two types, so conversion can be complicated. Whichever clutch the car has, make sure on the test run that it engages smoothly. Check for any clutch slip by accelerating in top gear whilst going uphill.

If the clutch inspection cover is wider than it is tall (as in this photo), it's probably a multi-plate clutch.

Gearbox   ④ ③ ② ①
If the idle speed is somewhat high, there may be some minor grinding of gears as first is selected – this is usually of no significance. Once under way, since the Model A has no synchromesh, unless driven by an experienced Model A driver some minor grating during gear changes is to be expected, particularly if the oil is cold. There may be some whine from the indirect gears of first and second, but there should be no untoward noises in top. Whilst descending a hill check for any jumping out of gear by using engine braking on the overrun. And also check that it does not slip out of second gear when ascending the hill. Slipping out of gear does not necessarily mean a gearbox rebuild; it may be simply a straightforward repair of the gearbox tower and its selector arms.
    If the car has an overdrive, check it is fully functional and engages easily.

Driving   ④ ③ ② ①
Listen for clunks from the suspension as you go over road irregularities. The Model A demonstrates very unstressed progress; the acceleration should be without hesitation or misfire, and it should pull well in top from a low speed. At 40mph it

should feel like it could go all day without fuss. The brakes need firm pressure, but should pull it up well without drama. The handbrake should only be used as a parking brake or an absolute emergency brake. If used whilst the car is in motion it is extremely effective, but so much so that it can bend its own mechanism! On the overrun there may be some back 'popple' from the exhaust. Unless severe, this is usually nothing to worry about.

The steering is heavy compared with modern cars, but generally good compared with its contemporaries. If you haven't ever ridden in a vintage car before, you will quickly become more aware of bumps and road camber.

Listen for any exhaust blow on acceleration.

You may hear a whine from the rear axle, but the Model A has a very robust rear axle assembly, and rarely do serious problems manifest. Once thoroughly warm, drive along in top gear at slow revs without labouring the engine, and as you accelerate by opening the throttle listen for any knocks from the engine, which could indicate main or big end wear. Whilst driving along take your foot off the throttle and look behind in your mirror for any signs of smoke indicating possible bore wear. Also try gently putting the power off and on with the throttle to check for any clunk from the universal joint or power train.

Check the speedo and odometer are working.

Obviously, unless you or your friend are actually driving the car, it's difficult to assess how good or bad the steering and handling are, but the Model A steers reasonably precisely compared with cars of a similar age. Cornering is usually undramatic and body roll is minimal (unless of course it's being driven with too much panache!).

At the end of the test drive

Park the car, but leave the engine running and reinspect the engine bay.

With the engine running, check the radiator, hoses and water pump are not leaking or overheating. Recoring a radiator is a straightforward job for a good radiator specialist.

Check no fuel is leaking from the fuel supply pipe, bowl or carburettor, and check for oil leaks of any significance. Often there is some minor seepage from the valve cover on the right hand side of the engine.

Under the car

Check the back of the engine. This is a renowned spot for Ford Model As to leak oil, and an occasional drip is to be expected, but not a gusher!

It is unlikely there will be any oil leaking from the gearbox, and similarly the back axle is usually problem-free. Oil or grease visible in this area is most likely simply to have been blown back from the engine or universal joint.

A two-blade fan was standard. Note minor damage to radiator fins.

Check the windshield wiper works.

Switch the engine off and on a few times to reassure yourself the starter and electrics are up to the job. When satisfied, turn off both the fuel supply and ignition.

Checking the interior
4 3 2 1

Feel the bottom of the fuel tank for any drips. The steering column is riveted to the tank, and this can sometimes be a source of leakage. Right from the outset it is good practice to make a habit of NOT utilising the steering wheel to heave oneself into the driver's seat! Repair of the fuel tank is expensive, as much of the car has to be dismantled to remove it.

Only the later models had the fuel tap in the engine bay: most As have the tap in the cabin at the bottom centre right of the tank, and some dampness at the tap may usually be discerned. Replacement taps and/or repair kits are available.

The dash panel is fitted to the fuel tank. In early cars it was nickel plated. Replacements are cheaper (but often poorer quality) than replating the original. The speedo was oval-shaped until late 1930, with a mileometer and trip mileometer in the housing. In late 1930, a revised dash appeared with a round speedo but no trip mileometer.

The speedos and mileometer on Ford As are rather fragile. Often, the speedo is working but the mileometer is not. Rebuilt speedos are available

Interior trim
4 3 2 1

As mentioned in chapter 7, check the seats, door panels and headlining again for any rips, staining or tears.

Most sedans had upholstery in various styles of cloth, and open cars mostly had artificial leather. By now, most cars have been re-upholstered, often with genuine leather, though this was originally fitted on only a few models. There is a plethora of upholstery kits available for all types of Model A Fords, in a wide choice of fabrics and styles.

Add-ons, accessories and extras
4 3 2 1

Henry Ford's policy was to sell a basic car, and encourage dealers to sell extras. Some Deluxe models had these options fitted as standard direct from the factory. Even today, there is a wealth of optional extras available for the Model A.

Sidemount spare wheels are popular, though they can limit access by restricting full opening of the front doors.

Rear luggage rack and trunk are useful.

Radiator stone guards can prevent rock damage to your pricey radiator.

Late 1930 Tudor. Fabric upholstery was generally used in the saloons.

Most As have had retrims by now.

'Wind Wings' can be fitted to the screen pillars.

'Wind Wings' – draft deflectors that affix onto the windshield pillars, making travelling with no side windows less blustery.

On the steering column are often mounted two supplementary gauges – a temperature gauge and an oil gauge. The Model A has a low oil pressure system, and generally runs at no more than 4psi. Running temperature is usually around 175 degrees Fahrenheit.

Period accessories can add charm and be useful at the same time.

Thermometers on the radiator cap look smart, but are often inaccurate.

Turn signals were not originally fitted.

Interior heaters are available, which fit to the manifold and draw warm air through a port in the bulkhead onto the knees.

Additional externally-mounted rear view mirrors are useful.

In place of the original radiator cap is often found a Quail mascot, sometimes combined with a radiator thermometer. Some cars have a 'Moto-meter' thermometer fitted to the radiator cap.

An oil fume extractor is sometimes fitted to the oil filler pipe in the engine bay.

Finally, be warned – whenever you buy a used car, no matter what make, and no matter how much it cost, soon after purchase you will encounter faults you were not previously aware of!

Evaluation procedure

Add up the total points.

Score: 92 = excellent; 69 = good; 46 = average; 23 = poor. Cars scoring over 64 will be completely usable and will require only maintenance and care to preserve condition. Cars scoring between 23 and 47 will require some serious work (at much the same cost regardless of score). Cars scoring between 48 and 63 will require very careful assessment of the necessary repair/restoration costs in order to arrive at a realistic value.

10 Auctions
– sold! Another way to buy your dream

Auction pros & cons
Pros: Prices will usually be lower than dealers or private sellers, and you might grab a real bargain on the day. Auctioneers have usually established clear title with the seller.

Cons: You have to rely on a sketchy catalogue description of condition and history. The opportunity to inspect is limited, and the biggest drawback is you cannot drive the car. Auction cars are often a little below par, and may require some work. The estimate is often priced unrealistically low, and it's easy to overpay if you get carried away by 'auction fever.'

Ask yourself why the car is being sold at auction. Sometimes owners want a quick sale, sometimes cars are being sold from a deceased person's estate. For vendors auctions may be preferred if the value of the car is difficult to gauge or pitch on the open market. Maybe unique features, special history or simply a rare model. Any reputable auction will make a full disclosure of known serious faults but of course there may be unknown ones awaiting discovery.

Which auction?
Auctions by established auctioneers are advertised in car magazines and on the auction houses' websites. The Model A Ford, not being a particularly valuable or rare car, quite often appears without much razzmatazz at local low-key auctions. A printed catalogue or a simple printed list of the lots for auctions might be available only a day or two ahead, though usually lots are listed and pictured on auctioneers' websites much earlier. Contact the auction company to ask if previous auction selling prices are available as this is useful information (details of past sales are often available on websites).

Catalogue, and entry fee to the auction venue
When you purchase the catalogue of the vehicles in the auction, it often acts as a ticket allowing two people to attend the viewing days and the auction itself. Catalogue details tend to be comparatively brief, but will include some history or ownership details of the car. It should certainly state the registration details whether all taxes due have been paid. It will also usually show a guide price to give you some idea of what you can expect to pay, and will tell you what is charged as a 'Buyer's premium.'

Payment details
Very carefully read all the pages of the catalogue well in advance and if you are unsure about anything at all contact the auctioneers to check. They are always helpful; they want to sell the vehicle as much as anyone.

The catalogue will also contain details of acceptable forms of payment. At the fall of the hammer an immediate deposit is usually required, the balance payable within 24 hours. If the plan is to pay by cash, there may be a cash limit. Some auctions will accept payment by debit card. Sometimes credit or charge cards are acceptable, but will often incur an extra charge. A bank draft or bank transfer will have to be arranged in advance with your own bank as well as with the auction house. No car will be released before all payments are cleared. If delays occur in payment transfers then storage costs can accrue.

Buyer's premium
A buyer's premium will be added to the hammer price: don't forget this in your calculations. It is not usual for there to be a further state tax or local tax on the purchase price and/or on the buyer's premium.

Viewing
In some instances it's possible to view on the day, or days before, as well as in the hours prior to, the auction. Do not even consider buying a car at auction unless you have at least inspected everything you can, including the engine, bodywork, interior and underneath as far as possible. If for any reason the auctioneers will not let you inspect the engine bay or interior you must suspect something is seriously wrong. While the officials sometimes may start the engine for you, or drive the vehicle onto the selling bay, a test drive is out of the question. Crawl under and around the car as much as you want, but it's unlikely the auctioneers will be willing to permit the car you are interested in be jacked up. You can also ask to see any documentation available, do so and verify their accuracy and legitimacy

Bidding
Before you take part in the auction, decide your maximum bid – and stick to it! And don't forget to factor in the buyer's premium; this can add a sizeable amount to the hammer price.

It may take a while for the auctioneer to reach the lot you are interested in, so use that time to observe how other bidders behave. When it's the turn of your car, attract the auctioneer's attention and make an early bid. The auctioneer will then look to you for a reaction every time another bid is made, usually the bids will be in fixed increments until the bidding slows, when smaller increments will often be accepted before the hammer falls. If you want to withdraw from the bidding, make sure the auctioneer understands your intentions – a vigorous shake of the head when he or she looks to you for the next bid should do the trick!

Assuming that you are the successful bidder, the auctioneer will note your card or paddle number, and from that moment on you will be responsible for the vehicle.

If the car is unsold, either because it failed to reach the reserve or because there was little interest, it may be possible to negotiate with the owner, via the auctioneers, after the sale is over.

Successful bid
There are two more items to think about. How to get the car home, and insurance. The auction house will normally hold the car for 24 hours, but after this may charge you a storage fee so you need to be ready to shift the car from their premises promptly. If you can't drive the car, your own or a hired trailer is one way, another is to have the vehicle shipped using the facilities of a local company. The auction house will also have details of companies specializing in the transfer of cars.

Insurance for immediate cover can usually be purchased on-site, but it may be more cost-effective to make arrangements with your own insurance company in advance, and then call to confirm the full details.

Online auctions could land you a car at a bargain price, or of course, they could land you with a wreck. You'd be foolhardy to make a legally binding bid without examining the car first, something most vendors encourage. A useful feature of eBay is that the geographical location of the car is shown, so you can narrow your choices to those within a realistic radius of home. Be prepared to be outbid in the last few moments of the auction. Remember, your bid is binding and that it may be difficult to get restitution in the case of a crooked vendor fleecing you – caveat emptor!

Many of the Model As advertised on eBay auctions do not sell at the immediate termination of bidding. Unless the purchaser has fully inspected and tested the car beforehand, the price reached often indicates, much to the vendors chagrin, the price the purchaser is willing to pay if the car is truly as described, including the engine. Undertake a road test if required, to endorse the accuracy of the advertisement.

Be aware that some cars offered for sale in online auctions are 'ghost' cars. Don't part with any cash without being sure that the vehicle does actually exist and is as described (usually pre-bidding inspection is possible).

Auctioneers

Barrett-Jackson www.barrett-jackson.com; **Bonhams** www.bonhams.com; **British Car Auctions (BCA)** www.bca-europe.com or www.british-car-auctions.co.uk; **eBay** www.eBay.com or www.eBay.co.uk; **H&H** www.handh.co.uk; **Manor Park Classics** www.manorparkclassics.com; **RM Sotheby's** www.rmsothebys.com; **Shannons** www.shannons.com.au;

11 Paperwork
– correct documentation is essential!

The paper trail

Classic, collector and prestige cars usually come with a large portfolio of paperwork accumulated and passed on by a succession of proud owners. This documentation represents the real history of the car and from it can be deduced the level of care the car has received, how much it's been used, which specialists have worked on it and the dates of major repairs and restorations. All of this information will be priceless to you as the new owner, so be very wary of cars with little paperwork to support their claimed history.

Registration documents (title)

All countries/states have some form of registration for private vehicles whether it's like the American 'pink slip' system or the British V5 system.

It is essential to check that the registration document is genuine, that it relates to the car in question, and that all the vehicle's details are correctly recorded, including frame/chassis/VIN and engine numbers (if these are shown). If you are buying from the previous owner, his or her name and address will be recorded in the document: this will not be the case if you are buying from a dealer.

In the UK the DVLA will provide available details of earlier keepers of the vehicle upon payment of a fee, but usually only those after about 1980.

If the car has a foreign registration there are several formalities to go through to get it street legal which can be time-consuming. If importing a car it is vital to have "Title" or other registration documentation from the exporting country. A car imported into the UK will have to go through the NOVA (Notification of Vehicle Arrival) process. Your national or local car club should be able to help guide you through the necessary legal procedures.

Roadworthiness certificate

Most country/state administrations require that vehicles are regularly tested to prove that they are safe to use on the public highway and do not produce excessive emissions. In the UK that test (the 'MoT') is carried out at approved testing stations, for a fee. In the USA the requirement varies, but most states insist on an emissions test every two years as a minimum, while the police are charged with pulling over unsafe-looking vehicles.

If the car has been entered in tours in the USA it is likely the owner will have completed and submitted roadworthiness inspection forms. Ask if copies of these are available. In the UK cars over a certain age (the Model A falls into this category) are exempt from compulsory annual MoT testing (a roadworthiness check). Many owners sensibly still submit their vehicles to this test or a similar one. Ask if the vehicle has had an independent roadworthiness check from a professional or other expert and if so ask to see the documents. Ask the seller if previous MoT certificates are available.

In New Zealand all motor vehicles require a periodic safety check (Warrant of Fitness). For vehicles first registered before 1954 the check is less rigorous but the vehicle should, within reason, conform to how it left the factory.

.

Road licence/tax

The administration of every country/state charges some kind of tax for the use of its road system. The actual form of the tax and how it is displayed varies enormously country to country and state to state.

Whatever the form of the licence, it must relate to the vehicle carrying it and must be present and valid if the car is to be driven on the public highway legally. The value of the licence will depend on the length of time it will continue to be valid.

In the UK if a car is untaxed because it has not been used for a period of time, the owner has to inform the licensing authorities (via the SORN system) otherwise the vehicle's date-related registration number will be lost and there will be a painful amount of paperwork to get it re-registered. Also in the UK, vehicles over 40 years old are taxed free of charge, but there is still annual renewal with the DVLA. Of course legislation and taxes can and do change, but a Ford Model A should last for ever!

Certificates of authenticity

For many makes of collectible car it is possible to get a certificate proving the age and authenticity (e.g. engine and chassis numbers, paint colour and trim) of a particular vehicle, these are sometimes called 'Heritage Certificates' and if the car comes with one of these it is a definite bonus. If you want to obtain one, the relevant owners' club is the best starting point.

If the car has been used in European classic car rallies it may have a FIVA (Federation International des Vehicules Anciennes) certificate. The so-called 'FIVA Passport', or 'FIVA Vehicle Identity Card,' enables organisers and participants to recognise whether or not a particular vehicle is suitable for individual events. If you want to obtain such a certificate go to <www.fbhvc.co.uk> or <www.fiva.org> there will be similar organisations in other countries too.

In New Zealand the Vintage and Veteran Car Club (VCC) will issue a Vehicle Identification Certificate (VIC) to specify a vehicle's authenticity; this document is required for entry into National Rallies, and is almost mandatory to re-register a vehicle after a period of lapsed registration.

Valuation certificate

It is unlikely the vendor will have a recent valuation certificate, or letter signed by a recognised expert stating how much he, or she, believes the particular car to be worth.

Though such a certificate may have been issued to get an 'agreed value' insurance. Such documentation is not a guarantee of value as the expert has probably not even seen the car in the flesh. The actual value of a Model A can only be truly assessed on the open market. The owners' club may be able to help you to obtain formal valuation but remember that it is not the same as market value!

Service history

Most Model As will have been serviced at home by enthusiastic (and hopefully, capable) owners for a good number of years. Nevertheless, try to obtain as much service history and other paperwork pertaining to the car as you can. Naturally, specialist garage receipts can be reassuring. Any relevant documentation can help. Items like the original bill of sale, original handbook, parts invoices and repair bills, add to the story and the character of the car. Good facsimile reprints of the cars' original handbooks are available from clubs and parts suppliers. If the seller claims that the car has been restored, then expect receipts and other evidence from a specialist restorer.

If the seller claims to have carried out regular servicing, ask what work was completed, when, and seek some evidence of it being carried out. Your assessment of the car's overall condition should tell you whether the seller's claims are genuine.

Restoration photographs

If the seller tells you that the car has been restored, then expect to be shown a series of photographs taken while the restoration was under way. Pictures taken at various stages, and from various angles, should help you gauge the thoroughness of the work. If you buy the car, ask if you can have all the photographs as they form an important part of the vehicle's history. It's surprising how many sellers are happy to part with their car and accept your cash, but want to hang on to their photographs! In the latter event, you may be able to persuade the vendor to get a set of copies made.

Make sure all documents match the car.

12 What's it worth?
– let your head rule your heart

Condition

If the car you've been looking at is really bad, then you've probably not bothered to use the marking system in chapter 9 – 60 minute evaluation. You may not have even got as far as using that chapter at all! If you did use the marking system you'll know whether the car is in Excellent (maybe concours), Good, Average or Poor condition or, perhaps somewhere in-between these categories.

Many classic/collector car magazines run a regular price guide. If you haven't bought the latest editions as well as researching on the internet, do so now and compare suggested values for the model you are thinking of buying: also look at any auction prices they're reporting. Values of all Model As have been slowly rising for several years, but some models will always be more sought-after than others. Trends can change, too. The values published in the magazines tend to vary from one magazine to another, as do their scales of condition, so carefully read the guidance notes they provide. Bear in mind that a car that is truly a recent prestigious show winner could be worth more than the highest scale published; here we are not talking about being "best in show" car at a local county agricultural event but more along the lines of a national Model A concours.

How does the average figure in magazines and internet sites compare with the asking price? Before you start any haggling with the seller, consider what effect any variation from standard specification might have on the car's value.

If you are buying from a dealer, remember the dealer is looking to make profit on the price, whether he has bought the car for cash or is selling it on commission.

Desirable options/extras

Many model As have one or more extras (originally even the spare tyre was an extra –though the spare wheel was included in the price). If complete originality is not being sought an extra that will significantly affect the value is an overdrive. Although hydraulic brakes might be considered desirable from a driving point of view they will often decrease the value of the vehicle rather than increase it.

Undesirable features

Any type of Model A with a modern or other non-standard engine, transmission or rear axle is best avoided. Many Model As have suffered at the hands of "Hot Rodders" this book is not for them. There is a world of difference between a true Model A Ford and a car that has been chopped, gutted and chromed into a Hot Rod.

Practically all Model As will have had replacement parts fitted at some stage, these should be to original pattern, anything else detracts from the cars desirability.

Striking a deal

Negotiate on the basis of your condition assessment, history/ownership record and fault rectification cost. Also take into account the car's specification. Be realistic about the value, but don't be completely intractable: a small compromise on the part of the vendor or buyer will often facilitate a deal at little real cost.

A photo history adds interest and heritage.

13. Do you really want to restore?
– it'll take longer and cost more than you think

Some people buy a 'project.' The main pleasure they get from the vehicle is working in the garage, fettling and assembling the components, leading to the day of celebration when, finally, the restored car is back on the road. Others derive pleasure from the joy of owning and driving a piece of automotive history. In between the two are the owners that undertake their own light restoration whilst still having the car driveable; the 'rolling restoration.'

Compared with modern vehicles, the Model A is a very easy car to work on. Practically all parts for it are available new from the specialist suppliers. Where new parts are not available, it is usually relatively straightforward to source used components through clubs or websites. Indeed, it is said that the parts availability these days is as good as it's been since the 1950s.

Fords can still come onto the market in rough condition having been stored in a barn or shed for years or decades. Many of these are vehicles on which restoration was begun, but the owner eventually lost interest or ran out of time.

A challenging but satisfying undertaking can be ahead of you bringing a sleeping beauty of a Model A back to life. Simple to strip down to basic pieces, it

A few years ago this Pick-up would have been restored; now it is more likely to be conserved as it is. (Courtesy John Charlton)

An unfinished restoration project is likely to have parts missing!

Restoration of a car requires at least a double garage. (Courtesy Richard Forsyth)

Restoration of the AA truck and its derivatives needs a vast amount of space. (Courtesy Russell Moore)

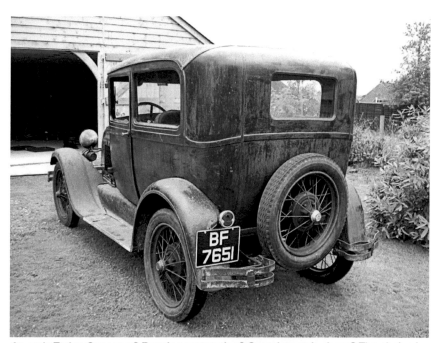

An early Tudor. Conserve? Running restoration? Complete strip down? The choice is yours. (Courtesy John Cochran)

is likely that every single one of these components requires working on, or you may decide the part is too far gone and use a new or used replacement. Beware of buying any old car that is in pieces: 'believed complete' is a phrase one sees all too often in adverts.

Also one of the unexpected things that catches out many home restorers is just how much physical space is required for all the parts of the car when it is disassembled and being worked on.

The cost of a complete professional restoration for a relatively cheap car such as the Model A does not usually

LHD pedals. Left to right: clutch, brake, accelerator, foot rest. (Courtesy Chris Thurley)

make financial sense. Generally, restorations involve the owner doing work within his competency and passing the rest to the professional.

Restoration of bodywork is probably the most time-consuming and expensive part of any project. The fenders and running boards of the Model A are bolted on, so their removal/replacement is straightforward. However, restoration of the bodyshell is usually beyond the scope of the amateur home enthusiast, and, like it or not, this task has to be farmed out to a professional.

Engine rebuilds probably necessitate re-babbitting (white metalling) the main and conrod bearings. Workshops capable of undertaking this are becoming rarer, so machining and installation of shell bearing is an option. Crank shaft regrind, reboring, and cracked block repair are other tasks usually delegated to professionals.

Once the professionals have finished their jobs on the car, reassembly is normally possible with just help from a few fellow enthusiasts.

The electrics are relatively simple for those with a basic understanding, and who are prepared to follow the wiring diagram closely.

Interior refurbishment (especially with one of the available upholstery kits) is within the realm of the home enthusiast who is prepared to spend time getting things just right.

Help in the form of books, videos, online advice and forums and other enthusiasts and clubs is abundant.

Wood replacement can be time-consuming on some models. (Courtesy Chris Thurley)

Chassis and engine completed; awaiting a body. (Courtesy Richard Forsyth)

Engine restoration is straightforward, but babbitt (white metalling) specialists are becoming scarce. Shell bearings can be fitted.

A Pick-up body waits to be lifted onto the chassis frame: then its ready for the open road. (Courtesy Mark Perkins)

Complete upholstery kits are available.

Removal of dust and grime may reveal a gem – or a disappointment.

Not all rebuilds are to concours standard.

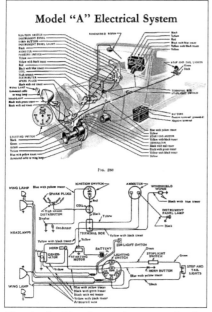

Simple electrics for any home mechanic.

Period advert: batteries last longer if kept fully charged.

14 Paint problems
– bad complexion, including dimples, pimples and bubbles

The paint finish can (and often does!) dominate one's first impression of a car. However, the lack of streamlining together with the overall design and character of a Model A makes paint perfection far less important than one would initially suppose.

If you miss bubbling paintwork this is what you'll find a year later.

People notice poorly fitting panels or doors before noticing a small paint blemish. Rusting chrome or nickel draws one's eye immediately, whilst a paint run may be almost inconspicuous.

Many enthusiasts now actively prefer the oily-rag vehicle, often choosing a car in 'hillbilly' condition rather than one (over)restored.

Paint defects are thus one of your lesser worries. The primary cost of bodywork restoration is repairing and fitting the panels and preparing them for the paint, rather than the actual paint spraying itself.

Beware of having it resprayed to too shiny a finish, which looks anachronistic and out of character.

Life is made easier by the fenders and splash shields above the running boards being black on every Model A worldwide. Wheels were black from 1927 to 1929. From 1930 onward, wheels came in a variety of colours depending on the colour of the body.

Shade selection
Selecting the correct shade of paint can present problems. Ford offered many colours, and on any car these will have faded over the years. Also, the colour inevitably varied from batch to batch, and the choice of colours offered was different from country to country. If the paint has faded and dulled and you wish to bring it back to shine, some proprietary paint restorers and/or paint cutting/rubbing compounds will retrieve the situation. As always, try it on an inconspicuous spot first and progress panel by panel.

Cracking

Many Ford As have suffered cracking paint around the fuel filler cap, where the weight of the fuel hose nozzle has been allowed to flex the metal. This is also an area where the paint may be stained from fuel drips. Paint restorer/rubbing compound and polish often gets rid of the stain.

Age-related crazing

If the car is aged, and particularly if it has been exposed to strong sunlight for a long period, general micro-crazing of the paint may be apparent. If you want to get the paint back to glossy factory-fresh, a respray will be needed.

Corrosion of underlying metal may manifest as paintwork blistering or bubbling. Things usually are worse than they appear; the metal will require repair before repainting.

Other problems are the usual ones associated with poor preparation or spray painting technique: 'Orange peel' which can sometimes be resolved with a rubbing compound, elbow grease and polish, but general cracking, micro blistering, peeling, dimples, if present throughout the vehicle, necessitate a complete respray if the wish is to restore to showroom condition.

The cracks around the filler cap here are not structural, but purely a paint problem.

Fender edges inevitably suffer.

15 Problems due to lack of use
– just like their owners, Ford Model As need exercise

Cars, like humans, are at their most efficient if they exercise regularly. A drive of at least ten miles, once a week, is recommended. Just starting the engine for a few minutes is bad practice. Laying up the car for an entire winter or longer without taking precautions can cause problems.

Seized components
The clutch may seize if the plate becomes stuck to the flywheel. Similarly, the emergency brake can seize onto the drum.

The brake system can seize, especially if damp and it has not been greased correctly.

Wheel bearing and water pumps can seize or become pitted if water displaces the grease.

Pistons can seize in the bores due to corrosion especially if water has entered the engine.

Fluids
Old, acidic, oil can corrode bearings.

Uninhibited coolant can corrode internal waterways. Lack of antifreeze can cause cracks in the block or head. Silt settling and solidifying can cause subsequent overheating.

Clubs are an invaluable source of help and support.

Fuel is an increasing problem. Modern fuels containing ethanol can degrade within a matter of weeks. In a damp environment they can absorb water and cause problems with the tank. Additives can help.

Tyre problems
Tyres that have had the weight of the car on them in a single position for some time will develop flat spots, resulting in some (usually temporary) vibration. If the tyre deflates completely and is left that way, a new inner tube and a new tyre are likely to be required.

Electrics
The battery will be of little use if it has not been charged for many months.

Grounding (earthing) problems are common when the connections have corroded. Old bullet and spade type electrical connectors commonly rust/corrode and require disconnecting, cleaning and protecting with dielectric grease, Vaseline or similar.

Storing cars in damp garages can cause problems to the starter motor and generator as well as speeding up corrosion of any connectors or contacts.

Bodywork
Long-term storage in damp sheds promotes general rusting. Try not to put your A away without drying it off if it's been on a damp run. Always let air circulate around the garage as much as possible on any dry day.

Rotting exhaust system
Exhaust gas contains a high water content, so exhaust systems corrode very quickly from the inside when the car is not used.

16 The Community

– key people, organisations and companies in the Model A world

Clubs

USA

Model A Ford Club of America www.mafca.com
Model A Restorers Club www. model-a-ford.org
Both of these clubs have many chapters in the USA and abroad.

Canada

Model A Owners of Cananda Inc. www.modelaowners.com

Europe

Model A Ford Cub of Great Britain www.mafcgb.org.uk
Sweden - Svenska A Fordarna www.afordarna.se
Norway – Norsk A Modell Klubb www.fordaklubb.no
Denmark – Dansk Ford A Klub www. dfak.dk
              Vamdrup Ford A Klub www.forda.dk
Netherlands – A Ford Club Nederlands www.a-ford.nl.

South America

Argentina www.clubamigosforda.com.ar

Australia

Model A Ford Club of South Australia http://www.mafcofsa.epizy.com
Model A Ford Club of NSW www.modelafordclubofnsw.com.au
Model A restorers Club of WA www.modelafordclub.com.au

New Zealand

North Island Model A Ford Club Inc www.modelafordclub.co.nz
MAFCA Canterbury Chapter www.modelaford.co.nz

On-line forums

Most of the clubs have a forum for members and some for non-members too.
Recommended are:
www.fordbarn.com
www.fordgarage.com
www.ahooga.com
www.plucks329s.org
www.fmaatc.org Ford Model AA Truck Club
www.aa-fords.com AA Truck forum

Service and parts suppliers

USA

Brattons www.brattons.com
Macs Antique Auto Parts
www.macsautoparts.com

A club day out.
(Courtesy Richard Forsyth)

A club run. Left to right: 1928 Tudor, 1930 Sorts Coupé, 1930 Coupé.
(Courtesy Jon Davidson)

Mike's 'A' Ford-Able Parts www.mikes-afordable.com
Snyders Antique Auto Parts www.snydersantiqueauto.com
There are many other suppliers in the USA, too.

UK
Belcher Engineering Ltd www.belcherengineeringltd.co.uk
O'Neill Vintage Ford www.oneillvintageford.co.uk

Australia
Henry's T and A parts https://henrystaparts.com.au

Recommended workshop technical manuals
Ford Model A Mechanics Handbook Volume 1 by Les Andrews.
The Complete Model 'A' Ford Restoration Manual by Les Pearson.
The Beginners Guide to The Ford Model A by Les Pearson.
Judging Standards and Restoration Guidelines published by MAFCA and MARC.

An extensive selection of books about the Model A Ford and copies of original Ford
Model A parts list and handbooks are available from the various clubs and suppliers.

As stated, the Model A was built globally. Many minor variations appeared in foreign assembly plants, where smaller components such as lights, glass, even carburettors were often sourced from local suppliers. Wherever the plant was – stateside or overseas – existing obsolescent components already in the parts bin would be used up before fitting the updated version. Even after 1931, production of Model A car and commercial vans and AA trucks continued in many countries.

General data
• Average sedan car dimensions:
• Length – 155in
• Height – 73in
• Width – 76in
• Tread (Track) – 56in
• Wheelbase – 103½in
• Weight – around 2350lb
• Rear axle ratio originally 3.7:1 until mid 1928, when it went to 3.78. Replacement gear and pinion sets are available now in the ranges 3.78:1, 3.54:1, 3.27; 4.11:1.

The Model A and Model B engines
Both are four-cylinder, side valve engines.
• Capacity – 200.5in^3 (3285cc)
• Firing order – 1243
• Compression ratio Model A – 4.22
• Bore – 3.875in
• Stroke – 4.25in
• Max power – Model A std engine, 40bhp at 2200rpm
           Model B std engine, 50bhp

Variation from the standard engine for the small-bore engine (other variations from standard with this engine were the carb and manifold specification):
• Capacity – 2043cc
• Bore – 3.05in
• Max power – small bore model A engine, 30bhp at 2600rpm
           small bore model B engine, 40bhp
• Small bore engine cars had a rear axle ratio of 4.55:1.

    Panel/delivery vans came in a selection of wheelbases – either car-chassis based with 103½in, or AA truck based with 131.5 or 157in.
    AA trucks could be either a swb of 131.5in, or lwb of 157in. The early ones had the same gear box as the car, the later ones had four forward gears. Their brakes were substantially stronger and had a larger braking surface area than the car version. The front suspension was similar to, but stronger than that in the car. The rear suspension was exceptionally strong cantilever springs.
    The early AAs had worm drive rear axle, changing in 1929 to bevel gears. They generally had 20in wheels. Trucks and vans and other commercials vehicles had

black radiator surrounds, except for the later deluxe vans, which had stainless steel surrounds like the cars.

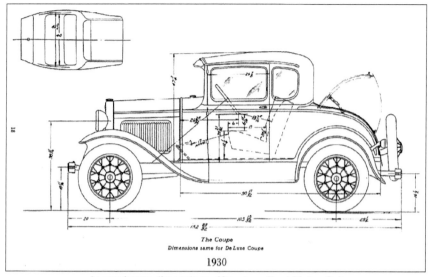

The Coupe
Dimensions same for De Luxe Coupe
1930

Approximate dimensions. (Courtesy Ford Motor Co)

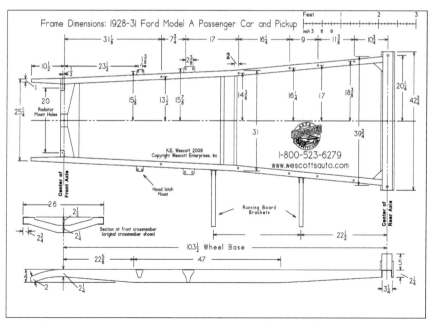

Restyling. Approximate chassis dimensions. (Courtesy Wescotts Auto)

INSTRUCTIONS

This lubricating chart gives full information for lubricating the MODEL A FORD. Proper lubrication has a vital effect on the life of the car. Consequently you should follow these instructions very carefully.

Each MODEL A came equipped with a pressure gun. By means of this device, lubricant can be forced under high pressure into all bearings provided with conical shaped fittings. To fill gun remove top cap and plunger assembly. Fill the barrel with lubricant, pack the lubricant solidly. Fill only to the top of the lettering on the outside of the barrel.

COMPRESSOR LUBRICATING GUN

(A) Lubricate every 500 miles. (Pressure gun). Use Number two high pressure lubricant in all high pressure lubricating fittings.

(B) Every 500 miles lubricate water pump shaft through water pump lubricating fitting, use water pump grease. (Pressure gun).

(C) Every 2000 miles remove the plug on the top of the steering gear housing and add gear lubricant, (600W), until it reaches the level of the filler plug hole. Never use high pressure lubricant in the steering gear.

(D) Every 1000 miles put two or three drops of oil in the front oil hole of the generator. The front oil hole is protected by a small cover. Do not put more than the recommended amount of oil in the oil hole as there is a possibility of oil getting on the brushes and affecting the operation of the generator.

(E) Every 2000 miles fill the oil cup at the rear of the generator. This is fed by a felt to the rear bearing.

(F) Every 5000 miles repack front wheel bearings with a short fiber sodium soap grease having a high melting point.

(G) Every 500 miles put a few drops of oil in oil holes at each end of the accelerator control shaft.

(H) Make sure radiator is kept filled with clean fresh water (a good anti-rust and water pump lubricant is suggested). During the winter in extremely cold areas be sure and use a good anti-freeze solution.

MODEL A

(I) Every 500 miles put oil in the oil cup at the side of the distributor. Add sufficient oil to reach the level of the oil cup.

(J) Every 2000 miles remove the distributor cap, clean lobes of the cam and apply a thin film of vasoline. The distributor should be kept clean and well oiled.

For the best tire life keep both front and rear tires inflated to 35 pounds. (On the station wagon or pick-up truck keep tires inflated to 40 pounds.) Note: When mounting spare, (side mount or in the rear), always put valve stem at the top as illustrated above.

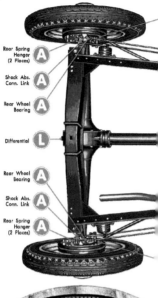

Rear Spring Hanger (2 Places) **(A)**

Shock Abs. Conn. Link **(A)**

Rear Wheel Bearing **(A)**

Differential **(L)**

Rear Wheel Bearing **(A)**

Shock Abs. Conn. Link **(A)**

Rear Spring Hanger (2 Places) **(A)**

(K) Lubricate every 2000 miles. (Pressure gun). The clutch bearing. This is done by removing the hand hole and turning the bearing until the lubricating fitting is at the top to get at. Note: The clutch is a dry disc type clutch and be oiled.

(L) Every 5000 miles the lubricant in the differential should and the housing flushed with kerosene. New lubricant should then be added until it reaches the level of the oil the rear of the housing.

(M) About every 5000 miles the gear lubricant should be the transmission by removing the drain plug at the transmission case. The interior of the transmission thoroughly flushed with kerosene, and refilled with fresh (600W). The new lubricant is poured into the transmission filler hole, located at the right hand side of the transmission enough lubricant in until it reaches the level of the filler h

(N) Every 500 miles change the motor oil. All internal lubricated from the oil reservoir in the oil pan by splash, and gravity feed. Only high grade motor oil shou the engine. During winter months a light grade of oil hav test is a must for the proper lubrication of the engine. SA winter, and SAE 40 weight oil for summer are suggested. be warm before draining.

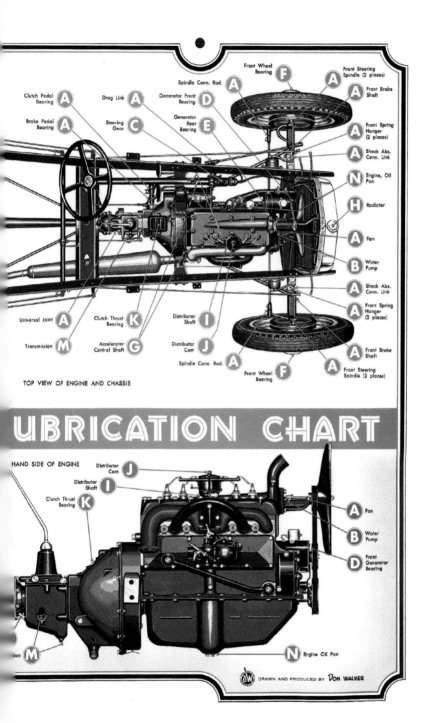

Front Wheel Bearing **F**

Front Steering Spindle (2 places) **A**

Spindle Conn. Rod. **A**

Front Brake Shaft **A**

Clutch Pedal Bearing **A**

Drag Link **A**

Generator Front Bearing **D**

Brake Pedal Bearing **A**

Steering Gear **C**

Generator Rear Bearing **E**

Front Spring Hanger (2 places) **A**

Shock Abs. Conn. Link **A**

Engine, Oil Pan **N**

Radiator **H**

Fan **A**

Water Pump **B**

Shock Abs. Conn. Link **A**

Front Spring Hanger (2 places) **A**

Universal Joint **A**

Clutch Thrust Bearing **K**

Distributor Shaft **I**

Transmission **M**

Accelerator Control Shaft **G**

Distributor Cam **J**

Front Brake Shaft **A**

Spindle Conn. Rod. **A**

Front Wheel Bearing **F**

Front Steering Spindle (2 places) **A**

TOP VIEW OF ENGINE AND CHASSIS

LUBRICATION CHART

HAND SIDE OF ENGINE

Distributor Cam **J**

Distributor Shaft **I**

Clutch Thrust Bearing **K**

Fan **A**

Water Pump **B**

Front Generator Bearing **D**

Transmission **M**

Engine Oil Pan **N**

DRAWN AND PRODUCED BY DON WALKER

59

Also from Veloce –

A veteran motoring journalist's extraordinary life, told through delightfully eccentric stories and charming diary extract. This unique book is packed with fascinating stories about classic cars and motorcycles, set in a bygone world, and properly fixed in time. (Fiction)

ISBN: 978-1-845848-44-6
Paperback • 21x14.8cm • 288 pages • 5 b&w pictures

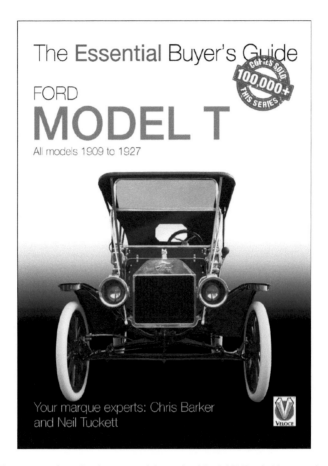

Index